What Do You Think?

Is Nuclear Power Safe?

John Meany

Heinemann Library
Chicago, Illinois

Editorial: Andrew Farrow and Rebecca Vickers
Design: Steve Mead and Q2A Solutions
Picture Research: Melissa Allison
Production: Alison Parsons

Originated by Chroma Graphics Pte. Ltd.
Printed and bound in China by Leo Paper Group

12 11 10 09 08
10 9 8 7 6 5 4 3 2 1

ISBN: 978-1-4329-0357-2 (hardback)

Library of Congress Cataloging-in-Publication Data
Meany, John.
  Is nuclear power safe? / John Meany.
    p. cm. -- (What Do You Think?)
  Includes bibliographical references and index.
  ISBN 978-1-4329-0357-2 (hardback : alk. paper) 1. Nuclear
engineering. 2. Nuclear energy--Safety measures. I. Title.
  TK9145.M43 2007
  363.17'99--dc22
                                        2007018229

Acknowledgments
The author and publishers are grateful to the following for permission to reproduce copyright material:

©Alamy p. 18 (David R. Frazier Photolibrary, Inc.); ©Corbis pp. 48, 15 (epa/Gildas Raffenel), 22 (Gabe Palmer), 35 (George D. Lepp), 24 (Karen Kasmauski), 45 (Reuters/Aziz Haldari), 10 (Reuters/Herwig Prammer), 46 (Reuters/Morteza Nikoubazi), 4, 30, 38 (Roger Ressmeyer), 32 (Sygma/Igor Kostin), 21 (zefa/Guenter Rossenbach); ©Masterfile p. 16 (Rolf Bruderer); ©NHPA p. 29 (B&C Alexander); Courtesy of Oregon State University Libraries p. 8; ©PhotoEdit Inc. p. 50 (Michelle Bridwell); ©Science Photo Library pp. 37 (RIA Novosti), 40, 43 (US Department of Energy); ©UPPA pp. 7, 26, 27 Photoshot, 13 (Photoshot/Landov/Bloomberg News).

Cover photograph: Cover photo of radioactive sign reproduced with permission of ©Alamy/Blackout Concepts.

The publishers would like to thank Dr. Roger Kingdon for his comments in the preparation of this title.

Every effort has been made to contact copyright holders of any material reproduced in this book. Any omissions will be rectified in subsequent printings if notice is given to the publisher.

Table of Contents

Some words are shown in bold, **like this**. You can find out what they mean by looking in the Glossary.

> *A nuclear future?*
Governments and electric power companies are now considering building a substantial number of new nuclear power plants. Public concerns about nuclear safety may interrupt development of future nuclear options.

Is Nuclear Power Safe?

On Tuesday, November 21, 2006, 1,800 students were evacuated from Tennessee schools because instruments at the Watts Bar Nuclear Plant showed a possible leak of radioactive water from the plant's cooling system. Plant operators declared an "unusual event"—the lowest of four emergency alerts for nuclear accidents in the United States. Although there was no proof that anyone was harmed or in danger, this was the 20th unusual event at a U.S. nuclear facility in 2006. Any such event raises public concerns about the dangers of nuclear energy plants, including radiation poisoning, accidental explosion, and core meltdown. Events like this one make nuclear power the subject of much debate. Many people hold strong opinions on both sides of this controversial issue.

Other energy sources also have their own risks and costs. **Fossil fuels** are plentiful and inexpensive, but coal, oil, and natural gas produce air pollution and **greenhouse gas** emissions that contribute to global climate change. Alternative and **renewable** energy sources, such as wind turbines, solar power, and hydroelectric power, are expensive and cannot be built quickly enough to keep up with the world's increasing demand for electricity. It may be that decades of successful use make nuclear power the most reliable option for meeting future electrical needs.

Why do we need nuclear power?

Nuclear power is a way to produce electricity. The world's energy needs are increasing and there is more demand for electricity. This is happening for two main reasons:

Society is more energy-intensive than in the past.

Simply put, each person today uses more energy than that same person might have 30, 50, or 100 years ago. A single person in an industrialized country today uses more than ten times the energy of a person from 1900. What are some of the reasons that people today use more energy?

There has been a dramatic and increasing consumer use of private automobiles, home appliances, such as dishwashers, microwave ovens, and laundry washers and dryers, and personal electronic and communication devices, such as televisions, computers, DVD and video recorders, digital cameras, CD and MP3 players, mobile phones, and PDAs. More businesses and homes have air conditioning and central heating systems. More people commute to work over longer distances, using electric bus or train services. Corporations use robotic and other advanced electronic technology.

Developing countries have expanding economies.

As countries add more industries, their energy needs increase. Each factory needs fuel and electricity to operate. More factories mean more factory workers. The workers have more income, which they use to purchase products that use electricity. This is especially a problem in large communities. China and India are the world's most populous countries, each with more than one billion people. They have had significant economic growth for the past 25 years and will have more in the future. Their populations are making more money

> *Nuclear reactor room*
>
> **This reactor room is in a nuclear power plant in Russia. Plants like this can contribute to the energy needs of a country.**

and buying more high-energy-use products. More than 400 million Indians do not yet have regular access to electricity—when they demand it, this will create a need for more fuel and electricity. The International Energy Agency expects China and India to double their energy use by 2030.

As demand for electricity increases, people will explore different sources to access this power. The current major source of electric energy is coal. Unfortunately, coal is not a clean fuel. Its use increases air pollution emissions and greenhouse gases. This pollution has short-term health effects, such as asthma and lung illnesses. Coal use also has the potential for catastrophic long-term environmental damage, because it increases the amount of greenhouse gas in the global atmosphere. Environmentalists, some governments, and the public are showing support for cleaner energy. As people, businesses, and governments search for cleaner energy sources to meet the world's future electrical needs, nuclear power appears to be a reasonable option.

Growing demand for energy

Although some countries have low energy use now, their economies and energy use are increasing rapidly. If Indian and Chinese people adopt lifestyles like Canadians, Americans, and Australians, there will be a significant increase in world energy needs.

This chart shows the amount of energy use per person in various countries.

The units used are kilograms of oil equivalent (kgoe) per person. One kilogram is approximately 2.2 pounds.

Country	kgoe	Country	kgoe
Canada	8,301	Turkey	1,106
United States	7,795	Panama	836
Australia	5,723	Egypt	761
Russian Federation	4,423	Zimbabwe	744
United Kingdom	3,918	Vietnam	539
South Africa	2,597	India	512
Jamaica	1,545	Bolivia	504
China	1,138		

[Source: International Energy Agency Statistics Division, 2006]

> *Popular culture and the atomic bomb*
>
> The fear of the atomic bomb and nuclear energy was a popular subject in U.S. comic books during the 1950s and 1960s.

The controversial history of nuclear power

Physicist Enrico Fermi created the first nuclear chain reaction in December 1942, during World War 2. The Allies, including Great Britain, Australia, the United States, and the Soviet Union, feared that Germany might be working on an atomic bomb to win the war. So Great Britain and the United States teamed up on the "Manhattan Project" and made an atomic bomb of their own. On July 16, 1945, these scientists successfully tested the first nuclear bomb.

Then, on August 6, 1945, as part of an effort to quickly end World War II in the Pacific, a U.S. plane dropped the first nuclear weapon on the Japanese city of Hiroshima. Three days later another nuclear bomb was detonated over the Japanese city of Nagasaki. The Japanese announced their surrender on August 15. About 230, 000 people died from the bombs and their after effects. These are still the only times nuclear weapons have been used in a war.

In the 1940s and 1950s, people feared the destructive power of "the bomb." Books and films, such as *Godzilla* (1954), *Tarantula* (1955), and *The Incredible Shrinking Man* (1957) explored the frightening effects of nuclear radiation. Real events scared the public, too. In 1959 a test reactor in Southern California had a 30 percent reactor core meltdown, releasing radioactive gases into the surrounding communities. Military aircraft with nuclear weapons crashed in Canada, Spain, Greenland, and the United States.

Government leaders thought that safe civilian use of nuclear energy might reduce the public's fears. In 1953 U.S. President Dwight D. Eisenhower spoke to the United Nations. His "Atoms for Peace" speech (see page 43) explained that using **uranium**-fueled nuclear power might offer future economic growth for everyone. The first nuclear plant opened 15 years after Fermi had made the first nuclear **chain reaction**.

How does nuclear energy work?

The **atom** is a building block of nature. It is the smallest part of an **element** that still retains its chemical properties. An atom consists of a dense nucleus of protons and neutrons surrounded by electrons. Atoms are extraordinarily small. A 150-lb. (68-kg.) human has about 7×10^{27} atoms (7 followed by 27 zeros, or 7,000,000,000,000,000,000,000,000,000). However, they are held together with large amounts of energy. The nucleus of an atom can be divided, releasing some of this energy. Splitting an atom is called **fission**.

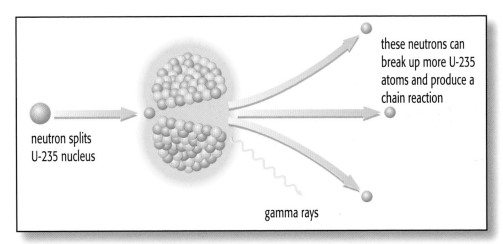

these neutrons can break up more U-235 atoms and produce a chain reaction

neutron splits U-235 nucleus

gamma rays

> *Nuclear fission*

This diagram shows the start of a nuclear fission chain reaction. It is the chain reaction that makes it possible to obtain a continual supply of energy from uranium.

In a nuclear power plant, uranium atoms continually collide and split. This chain reaction produces heat, which is used to turn water into steam. This complex process is generally similar to using stove controls to adjust the temperature of water. The steam power produced is used to turn turbines, machines with blades that rotate to generate electricity. Electric power lines then deliver this electricity to factories, cities, and homes.

> *The nuclear power debate*

Here the International Atomic Energy Agency is shown discussing Iran's development of a nuclear program. The consequences of a country choosing to use nuclear power can affect the whole world. It could provide energy independence for many countries and reduce pollution. It also produces dangerous radioactive waste and might lead to more nations having nuclear weapons. Students debating this subject need to know the advantages and disadvantages of this technology.

Thinking And Debating Skills

Good communication skills help people share their ideas, participate in important discussions, and develop self-confidence. These skills include effective public speaking, research and writing, argumentation, and **refutation**. With these tools, a person should be able to select the best topic, organize a speech or essay, make persuasive **arguments**, defend the arguments, and entertain or hold the interest of readers or listeners.

The best communicators are able to combine the elements of persuasion and argumentation. Persuasion is the effect that the style of presentation has on a listener. For a speaker, persuasion involves speaking clearly, with sufficient volume. Persuasive speakers use their voices to capture an audience's attention. They emphasize some words or phrases more than others, changing the tone. A writer does the same but uses words on paper to deliver simple and direct messages. Both speakers and writers present carefully organized ideas to explain their thoughts about an issue.

To convince others who hold different opinions, a person must persuade them to pick the best idea, the one that does less harm or gets the greater benefit. A skilled speaker should be able to change opinions, reduce conflict, and gain cooperation. For that, a person must be able to use effective arguments and debate.

Making an argument

Most people do not like to have arguments. Arguing is a negative experience that can be stressful, emotional, or upsetting. Many people associate an argument with a personal disagreement, but it is much more than that.

So what is an argument? It certainly includes a statement of an opinion, but it also adds more. An argument is the statement of an opinion that is supported by reasoning and evidence. An argument has three parts:

1. The **A**ssertion
2. The **R**easoning
3. The **E**vidence

You may remember this with the code **A – R – E**.

> *Supporters and opponents of nuclear power*
>
> There have been passionate debates on nuclear power and nuclear weapons for decades, many of them taking place in the General Assembly of the United Nations, shown here. Some debaters use the argumentation techniques listed in this book, while other speakers use emotion to appeal to the audience. Highly effective speakers often mix reasoning and emotion. Which techniques do you think would work for different audiences?

The first part of an argument is an assertion, or the brief statement of an opinion. It is the topic of the argument—a fact or claim that a complete argument proves. Examples of assertions include:

I am cold.

Dogs make the best pets.

Video games are too violent.

Bicycling uses less energy than walking.

Sports help bring the world together.

Too many people go hungry.

Nuclear power reduces air pollution.

The second step of an argument is reasoning. Reasoning is the explanation of an assertion. It provides the logic, the critical thinking, and the analysis of the argument. Reasoning answers the question: WHY? Why are you cold? Why do dogs make the best pets? Why do you think video games are too violent? If there is no reasoning for an argument, speakers will not be able to explain why their opinions are better than any other opinions.

The third and final step in making an argument is evidence. Evidence is factual support for your reasoning. Like evidence in a court of law, it is the information that supports the story of the witness or speaker. Evidence can include factual material, general statistics, historical examples, current events and examples, expert testimonies, personal stories, and other resources that support reasoning. Evidence is convincing because these kinds of factual information can provide proof for a well-reasoned idea.

 Personal arguments

An argument is often understood to be an angry disagreement or personal conflict. Here is an example of this kind of arguing, which is often ineffective:

You (to a friend): Please don't take that. I think that is my CD.

Friend: No, it is mine. You borrowed it.

You: It's mine. I bought it.

Friend: It's mine.

You: I bought it last week.

Friend: No. You borrowed it from me.

You: Bought it.

Think about how A – R – E skills could be used in this kind of argument.

Refuting an argument

It is not enough simply to have arguments. A good debater must also be prepared to disprove any opposing arguments. The skill used to defeat the arguments of another person is called refutation. Refutation is the process of proving that a claim or argument is wrong. Effective refutation includes anticipating what an opponent will say, different types of replies, and a clear and direct disagreement. There are four good ways to refute an idea:

1. Test its relevance

A speaker may explain one or more reasons that a point is irrelevant to the issue that is being discussed. For example, one speaker may argue that nuclear power is safe because it is difficult for terrorists to succeed in an attack against it. However, it is not a direct reply to say that nuclear power is expensive. The cost of nuclear power has nothing to do with its security against terrorist attacks. The first speaker could refute the opponent by saying that cost is irrelevant to making a decision about safety.

2. Examine its significance

A speaker can refute an opponent's point by showing that his or her own argument is more important. Not all arguments are equal—some matter more than others. Two important kinds of significance are qualitative and quantitative. Qualitative significance shows the seriousness of an issue's impact, and quantitative significance shows the number of cases. If a nuclear power plant leaks radiation, could it poison a person (qualitative significance)? How many people are hurt by the leak (quantitative significance)? The public would be much more concerned about a significant radiation leak affecting tens of thousands of people than about mild exposure for one person. To use this strategy for effective refutation, a successful debater tries to increase the significance of his or her own arguments, explaining why these arguments matter a great deal, while trying to reduce the significance of opposing points.

3. Capture it

A speaker may capture another's points by proving that opposing points actually prove his or her case. For example, a speaker might argue against nuclear power because it causes radiation pollution. A person arguing for nuclear power might reply by saying, "You are right—it is important to stop radiation pollution. But coal mining and burning causes more radiation pollution than uranium mining and nuclear energy. And if countries do not increase nuclear power, they will increase the use of coal, making radiation pollution worse." In this example, the effective debater has used the argument about radiation pollution to support the case for nuclear power.

> *Arguing for and against nuclear power*

Many environmentalists are concerned about the development of nuclear power, because of the problems of nuclear waste and terrorism. But within the environmental movement, some organizations and individuals now support nuclear development. More concerned with **global warming** than radioactive waste, they now argue against more traditional environmental protestors who have opposed nuclear power for decades.

4. Answer it

If an opponent makes an effective argument that you cannot capture, then you must answer it by producing your own reply, using the argument formula, A – R – E.

> *The nighttime skyline of Shanghai, China*

In the next 25 years, the world will need 50 percent more energy and electricity than is used today. The largest electricity growth will occur in Asia. With nearly half the planet's population, there will be a substantial need for new sources of energy for factories, offices, transportation networks, and modern communications.

What Are The Costs Of Nuclear Power?

Do you have lighting? Air conditioning? A refrigerator, toaster, or microwave oven? Telephone, computer, video game system, or DVD player? These products or services use electricity, which is produced by using fuel to generate electrical charges. Coal, oil, natural gas, nuclear, solar, wind, hydroelectric, and biomass are popular fuel sources. People pay for electricity the same way they pay for food, housing, and clothing. The price of electricity can be quite cheap or very expensive.

According to the United Nations, more than two billion people do not have electricity. Many of them live in countries like India and China, which are rapidly becoming global economic powers. As the citizens of these countries earn more money, they will demand many of the products and services that are available in the industrialized world, including products that use more energy.

The cost of electricity matters a great deal. If the price is too high, few businesses or individuals will be able to afford it. The economy will not grow, and people will not have access to new technologies that might improve the quality of their lives. If the price of electricity is too low, people may use too much electricity. They might waste it and increase both air and water pollution.

Supply and demand

To understand the cost of nuclear power or electricity, or the price of any product or service, it is necessary to learn the basics of economics—**supply and demand**. The supply is the amount of a good or service that is available. If a person has 8 bananas, the supply is 8. If that person has 23 CDs, the CD supply is 23. The demand is the desire that people have for something. How many want it? If 8 people want bananas, then the demand is 8.

The price of any item is based on the relationship of supply and demand. If there is more supply than demand, the price will go down. If there is more demand than supply, the price will go up. Consider the example of the bananas. If a grocer has 8 bananas to sell and only 2 people want a single banana (more supply than demand, 8 > 2), the grocer will have extra bananas. Rather than have the bananas spoil, the grocer might lower the price to encourage more people to buy the bananas or might get the 2 interested customers to purchase more than 1 banana each. If there are 8 bananas to sell and 20 people each want a banana (more demand than supply, 8 < 20), the grocer will not have enough bananas for each interested person. The customers might be willing to pay more to get one of the few available bananas. The price might go up!

> *The economics of supply and demand*
>
> **With more supply of an item than demand for it, the price goes down. If there is more demand than supply, the price goes up. That is the reason that perishable or hard-to-find products, or scarce resources, are more expensive.**

The cost of nuclear power

The issue of supply and demand applies to nuclear power plants and electricity. Let's first consider the costs of nuclear power plant energy production. There are several major costs in making nuclear electricity. First, it costs between $3 billion and $9 billion to construct a nuclear power plant, depending on its size and location. There are other costs, such as buying uranium fuel, operating the plant (paying the workers), and cleaning the equipment. Millions of dollars are spent to reduce pollution, make the plant safe, and protect it from theft or terrorism. Nuclear power plants also produce radioactive waste that must be kept away from the public. The waste can be a danger for hundreds of thousands of years. It is expensive to keep it away from people for such a long time. In most countries, the government must help pay the cost to build and deliver nuclear power. It is too expensive for private energy companies to produce.

If other sources of energy are available and prices are low, there is not much reason for governments or electric power companies to produce more nuclear energy. The public will already have the energy it wants and needs. It would also cost billions of dollars to build a new nuclear power plant—the government or businesses could decide that it would be better to spend or invest that money on other needs like transportation, education, or health care.

Comparative projected prices for electricity in 2010

Things may change. These prices are in cents per kilowatt hour (kWh).

Country	Nuclear	Coal	Gas
Canada	2.60	3.11	4.00
Czech Republic	2.30	2.94	4.97
Finland	2.76	3.64	--
France	2.54	3.33	3.92
Germany	2.86	3.52	4.90
Japan	4.80	4.95	5.21
Korea	2.34	2.16	4.65
Netherlands	3.58	--	6.04
Romania	3.06	4.55	--
Switzerland	2.88	--	4.36
Slovakia	3.13	4.78	5.59
United States	3.01	2.71	2.67

[Source – Organization for Economic Co-operation and Development Nuclear Energy Agency/International Energy Agency, 2005]

How do you select a source of energy?

In some countries, there currently is no need for new kinds of energy. Saudi Arabia, with a small population and enormous oil supplies, has more energy than it needs. It does not need nuclear power. Some countries, however, do not have oil, coal, natural gas, or uranium resources. In these places, such as Japan and Finland, nuclear power is an important energy option.

Fossil fuels or nuclear power?

Coal, oil, and natural gas are fossil fuels. A fossil fuel is made of ancient plant and animal life. The carbon in these fuels burns and creates heat and energy. Unfortunately, burning carbon produces air pollution and greenhouse gases. India and China use their limited coal and oil resources to provide energy for their huge populations—more than a billion people each. Therefore, they have serious pollution problems and may need to find a cleaner, plentiful energy source to meet their growing energy needs. Nuclear power may be preferable to fossil fuels, depending on a country's location, economy, and amount of pollution.

Fossil fuels are relatively inexpensive, and the technology to produce electricity from them is well known. Coal is plentiful in the countries that need significantly more energy. The seven countries with the most coal are the United States, the Russian Federation, China, India, Australia, Kazakhstan, and South Africa. Coal power produces 80 percent of the electricity in Australia, 50 percent in the United States, and 34 percent in the United Kingdom.

The United States plans to build 100 new coal power plants, and China has ordered more than 500 coal-fired electricity plants. Because there is so much coal, it may be less expensive than nuclear power. Some experts believe that nuclear power might save money. On the chart on page 19, the projected costs for nuclear power show it as cheaper in seven of the countries included in their survey. Others think that nuclear power may be at least double the cost of coal in the United States and the United Kingdom, and three times higher than coal in Australia.

Nonrenewable and renewable energy

Fossil fuels are **nonrenewable** sources of energy—they cannot be replaced in our lifetimes. The world's uranium and coal supplies may last for hundreds of years, but oil and natural gas stores may last only a few decades. Many government officials, business leaders, and environmentalists want renewable energy instead.

Renewable energy can never be used up. Renewable energy includes solar, wind, water, and biomass (renewable growing sources, such as wood, sugarcane, and switch grass). Renewable energy is plentiful. Most forms provide clean, nonpolluting energy for the future. In Brazil, a new project, *Luz para Todos* (Light for All), provides electricity for more than 12 million people, much of it provided by renewable systems, such as solar and water energy.

> *The option of renewable energy*

The ideal energy source would be renewable, inexpensive, and clean. This would provide unlimited energy for personal and industrial energy needs but would not significantly add to the world's energy-related environmental crises. Renewable energies—solar, wind, hydroelectric, geothermal, and biomass—have the potential to revolutionize energy production.

Measuring electricity

Electricity is measured in **watts**, a unit named in honor of eighteenth-century Scottish engineer James Watt, the inventor of the modern steam engine. A kilowatt (kW) is 1,000 watts. The amount of electricity a power plant produces is measured in kilowatt-hours (kWh). This measurement is equal to the energy of 1,000 watts working for one hour.

How much electricity do you use? What does it cost? Your government energy department or electric company measures each home's electricity use each month. Check the electric rate that your family pays. Has your family used more electricity this year than last year? Does your family use more electricity in the summer or winter? What can your family do to reduce the amount of electricity it uses?

> *People can save energy*

Consumers can make lifestyle changes that can save energy. Walking, bicycling, and taking public transportation reduce the use of gasoline and electricity. Recycling garbage and avoiding waste reduces the energy that is required to make new products. Sports and outdoor activities reduce the use of television and video games.

Conservation of energy

Energy **conservation** can increase the amount of energy without increasing cost. Conservation encourages people to decrease their energy use. Conservation can include energy-efficient building designs, so that homes and businesses do not waste heating or air conditioning. For businesses and cities, it might mean reduced lighting or electric advertising at night. Conservation can also include simple lifestyle changes that anyone could do, such as simply remembering to turn off lights and appliances when leaving a room. Although the United States has only 5 percent of the world's population, it uses 26 percent of the world's energy. In fact, a typical American uses nine times more energy than the average in the rest of the world. And Americans do not use the most energy! Canadians use more energy per person than any other country. The United States is second. With better home and office design, more efficient appliances, and a reduction in electronic luxury items, people can save energy.

Is it better to save money and get more energy from conservation than to spend money on building more nuclear power plants? Nuclear power plants cost billions of dollars. The plants do save money over time, however, because of the low cost of nuclear fuel. There is a large worldwide supply of uranium, enough for more than 500 years. Uranium is also a more efficient heat source. The fission of a uranium atom produces 10 million times the amount of energy that comes from oxidizing an atom of carbon from coal.

New light bulbs

New types of light bulbs are now available that have a longer life and use less energy. They are compact fluorescent bulbs, also known as energy-saving or low-energy bulbs. Over the lifetime of a bulb, a compact fluorescent can save $30 in electricity costs in comparison to a standard incandescent (filament) light bulb. Some countries are making plans to phase out the use of incandescent bulbs. So far, Australia, parts of Canada, and the United Kingdom are moving in this direction.

> **_Coal is an environmental danger_**

One of the most plentiful energy sources is coal. It is also one of the most harmful to the environment. Strip mining, like this, destroys topsoil and contaminates the water. Water contamination is so severe that water is not only unfit for drinking but is unclean for industrial use.

What Are The Environmental Costs Of Nuclear Power?

Each source of electrical energy has environmental advantages and disadvantages. Making electricity is unclean—it involves mining, burning fuels, and toxic waste. Energy production threatens land and water resources, plant and animal life, and human health and safety. Mining destroys the soil and creates chemical waste that poisons rivers and lakes. Burning fuel, particularly coal, to produce electrical energy can lead to serious air pollution problems. Nuclear power plants produce radioactive waste. Even renewable energy—solar, wind, hydroelectric, geothermal, and biomass—can cause environmental problems. For example, changing the course of a river to make a hydroelectric power plant can harm animal habitats. Burning biomass as a fuel source still releases pollutants into the atmosphere. In addition, manufacturing renewable energy equipment from metals and plastics produces air, water, and solid waste toxins.

For many years, most governments of more developed countries have tried to reduce energy pollution. But there is still significant smog and haze in the atmosphere above cities. Acids in rain and groundwater put marine life at risk. More importantly, air pollution can be deadly even when you cannot see it. The small particles of pollution from fossil fuels can cause asthma, lung disease, and even cancer.

Air pollution

The most common source of electrical production in the industrialized world is the coal-fired power plant. Most of these power plants were built in the 1950s and 1960s. Because they were built decades ago, countries' current pollution control laws do not apply to them. In the United States, many of the largest coal power plants do not have to follow the nation's toughest anti-pollution laws. Coal plants are responsible for the most harmful air pollutants. They release sulfur dioxide, nitrogen oxides, mercury, carbon monoxide, and carbon dioxide. Electrical energy production from coal gives off 38 percent of all U.S. carbon dioxide emissions. Worldwide, coal burning for electricity is responsible for 86 percent of total sulfur dioxide emissions, 90 percent of nitrogen oxides, and 75 percent of mercury emissions.

> *Fossil fuel pollution—a global threat*

In 2005, the World Health Organization estimated that more than 4 million people die each year from diseases caused by air pollution. A significant percentage of those are victims of the harmful gases from fossil fuel electricity production.

Effects of pollution

Sulfur dioxide is an acidic gas that contributes to acid rain. This environmental problem pollutes the water and poisons fish and marine mammals. Nitrogen oxide leads to smog and irritates lungs. It also increases the risk of bronchitis, asthma, and lung cancer. Carbon monoxide can increase the chance of heart

> *Coal threatens workers' health*

Coal mining is a dirty and dangerous business. Thousands of miners are killed each year in tunnel collapses, explosions, and fires. Millions of mine workers worldwide are at risk of "black lung," a disease that is caused by breathing coal dust.

disease and stroke. Mercury is a dangerous toxin that poisons the nervous system. In the United States, Canada, the United Kingdom, and Australia, it is estimated that 40,000 lives could be saved annually if the world lost the extra air pollution released by coal-fired electricity production.

Risks for workers

Nuclear power plants do not produce any of the gas pollutants that coal burning does. There are concerns, however, that nuclear power plants might release radiation. This could contaminate the air and cause lung and other cancers. In 2005, the U.S. National Academy of Sciences issued a report on the U.S. nuclear industry. It said that if nuclear industry workers were exposed to the national permitted annual levels of radiation during a long working career, up to 20 percent could develop cancer.

Global climate change

One of the most significant gases released during the burning of fossil fuels is carbon dioxide. The carbon dioxide in the atmosphere traps the heat from the sun and some of the heat that would leave Earth. This increases the temperature on the surface of Earth, much as in a gardener's greenhouse. That is the reason that carbon dioxide is known as a greenhouse gas.

For more than a century, people have increased fossil fuel use. This has led to a substantial increase in the amount of carbon dioxide in the atmosphere. Climate scientists have argued that the planet's temperature is increasing as a result of the buildup of carbon dioxide.

Effects of global warming

Flooding

Increased global warming could speed up the melting of polar ice, adding more water to Earth's oceans. The U.S. National Aeronautics and Space Administration (NASA) reported that polar ice caps are melting ten times faster than predicted. Scientists have argued that this melting would increase the sea level, flooding cities and towns on the coasts of countries throughout the world. More than 10 percent of the world's population could be affected directly—more than 650 million people live in coastal areas that are less than 33 feet (10 meters) above sea level. Urban areas at risk include many of the world's major cities: London, New York, Tokyo, Venice, and Buenos Aires. Within the century, the melting of polar ice could add 10 feet (3 meters) to the world's ocean levels. But even a much smaller change could seriously affect the planet. The Australian Government's Commonwealth Scientific and Industrial Research Organization released a study showing that just a three-foot (one-meter) increase would flood the city of Sydney. It would force 75 to 150 million people in Asia and the Pacific from their homes.

Weather changes

Global warming may also produce weather changes that will increase the number and intensity of hurricanes and storms. One recommendation to solve the problem is to substitute nuclear power for coal. Nuclear energy has been successfully used for 50 years, and it does not release any greenhouse gases. Opponents of nuclear power argue that it will take too long, perhaps several decades, to develop enough nuclear power to begin to replace coal. That might be too late to deal with the global warming crisis. Another factor is that although nuclear plants do not produce any greenhouse gases, uranium mining for nuclear fuel does produce significant greenhouse gas pollution.

> *Is it too late to stop climate change?*

Thousands of climate scientists throughout the world agree that climate change caused by human activity is underway. The ten warmest years ever recorded have occurred since 1995. Scientists have determined that climate change is increasing at a pace faster than they anticipated. But no one knows if the "tipping point" has been reached. This would mean that continuing negative changes were unstoppable.

Many environmentalists are in favor of energy conservation and increased use of renewable energy, like solar power. Some sources of renewable energy are clean, with no greenhouse gas emissions. However, supporters of nuclear electricity point out that even the combination of conservation and renewable energy will not provide enough electricity for the world's growing demand. These sources could meet only 20 percent of the world's energy needs. New technologies are also expensive. Therefore, for financial reasons, renewable technology may not be developed to meet the needs of billions of current and new electrical users.

Nuclear waste

Nuclear power may not significantly contribute to air and water pollution or greenhouse gases, but, like other kinds of chemical and industrial production, it does produce highly toxic waste. The most serious waste is called high-level waste. This material must be safely kept from humans and the environment for hundreds of thousands of years. The most dangerous waste of this type is spent fuel, which is the older, used uranium fuel from a nuclear reactor. Spent fuel is highly **radioactive**. Although it is only 3 percent of nuclear waste, it contains 90 percent of the radioactivity. It is usually kept at a nuclear power plant in cooling pools for several years and is later transferred to permanent storage or reprocessing.

> **> Old nuclear facilities created dangerous waste**
> Many nuclear power plants that began producing electricity 30–40 years ago are now reaching the end of their effective operations. When nuclear plants are decommissioned, or taken out of service, the radioactive equipment and fuel left behind is nuclear waste. This toxic material must be kept safely away from the public. In this picture, low-level nuclear waste is being dumped in drums in a trench in the state of Washington.

The United Nations' International Atomic Energy Agency believes the best option currently available is to store the waste underground. Other people worry that earthquakes, geological movement, terrorism, or accidents make underground storage of waste an unacceptable solution. In time, the waste might also escape into underground water supplies used for agriculture or city wells. At the present time, there is no permanent solution to the problem of storing this dangerous waste.

Reprocessing

Nuclear plant operators also reprocess nuclear fuel. **Nuclear reprocessing** is a chemical method to recycle some of the waste to be used again as fuel. The reprocessing of waste is so dangerous that it is banned in some countries, such as the United States.

Other waste

Coal, oil, and natural gas energy production also create **hazardous wastes** from the mining, drilling, transportation, and burning of fuel. Although it is dangerous, the waste from fossil fuels does not have to be protected for thousands of years. There is some waste from renewable energy sources. Biomass has to be burned, releasing carbon dioxide, along with nitrogen oxide and particulates. However, the problems associated with nuclear waste and fossil fuel waste are currently much greater.

What is radioactive half-life?

Radioactive half-life is the length of time it takes radioactive materials to decay. It measures the time needed for half of the material to have decayed to some other form. Here are half-lives for some radioactive materials found in nuclear waste:

Uranium 235: 713 million years

Uranium 238: 4.5 billion years

Plutonium 239: 24,000 years

Because of this continuing radioactivity, nuclear waste needs to be stored safely for hundreds of thousands of years.

> *The Soviet nuclear disaster at Chernobyl*

Chernobyl was the worst disaster in nuclear power history. Devastating explosions destroyed the roof of the Chernobyl reactor, allowing radioactive gas to escape into the atmosphere. The small radioactive particles released in the explosion later fell back to Earth and contaminated the area around the plant and even affected people in other countries.

How Safe Is Nuclear Power?

On April 26, 1986, a catastrophic meltdown occurred in one of four nuclear power reactors operating at the Chernobyl nuclear facility in the former Soviet Union (now in Ukraine). It was the worst nuclear accident in history. The reactor's core overheated, creating pressure that blew the roof off the reactor. The explosion destroyed the building and left 200 tons of highly radioactive waste. It released radioactive particles that spread across much of Europe, emitting radiation that affected more than 7 million people. The radiation was even found as far away as the United States and Canada. Nearly 400,000 people had to be evacuated from the area surrounding the power plant. The World Health Organization studied the results of the disaster. The organization concluded that 56 deaths resulted from the explosion and immediate exposure to radiation, while up to 9,000 cases of cancer developed from the accident's radioactive contamination.

At Chernobyl, the combination of a bad plant design, failure to correct safety problems, and worker errors resulted in disaster. The accident at Chernobyl made the public pay attention to the safety of nuclear power. Chernobyl led to better international control of nuclear power plants. The question is: Have the changes made nuclear power safe?

Safety issues

Human or mechanical error can cause a nuclear catastrophe. The most dangerous kind of accident is a **core meltdown**, in which the nuclear fuel overheats, destroying the nuclear power plant and releasing poisonous radiation into the air and ground. A core meltdown can injure or kill many thousands of people, contaminate land and water, force the evacuation of hundreds of thousands of people, and cost tens—even hundreds—of billions of dollars. It could poison an area of thousands of square miles for centuries.

Because of the seriousness of an accident, safety of nuclear power is of primary importance. Nuclear power is one of the most studied and regulated industries on the planet. To guarantee safety, nuclear power operators are required to use the best construction methods, with multiple back-up safety systems that identify problems and limit damage, and a thick concrete shield (3-5 feet/ 1-1.5 meters) over the nuclear core. Well-trained workers are also essential in maintaining safety.

Regulations and training

Government regulations and industry training have made nuclear power a generally safe industry. More than 30 countries have nuclear power plants—all of these plants added together have operated for a total of more than 12,000 combined years. In that time, there have been only two major accidents, both of which occurred in the 1970s and 1980s. Nuclear design and worker training has improved since then.

There may be more safety problems in the future. Most of the nuclear power plants working today were built in the 1960s and early 1970s. As the plants age, they are more at risk for accidents, just as people tend to suffer more accidents and illnesses as they age. Equipment cracks, wears out, and corrodes. In Sweden in 2006, four of the country's ten nuclear plants were closed due to cracks and mechanical failures.

In Japan, a 1999 accident at a nuclear fuel plant exposed workers to lethal amounts of radiation. A second accident at a Japanese reactor in 2004 killed five workers. Accident risks at two nuclear plants in the United Kingdom were so high that the Irish government appealed to the United Nations International Court to have the plants shut down. The equipment of the U.S. David–Besse nuclear power plant was so rusted that it could have caused a core reactor meltdown if the danger had not been discovered. The plant had to be closed for two years to make repairs. Many safety experts believe that the chance of an accident will only increase as more plants get older.

> *Three Mile Island—a near miss*
>
> **Although the power plant does not appear to have much external damage, the meltdown at Three Mile Island in 1979 was the second most dangerous nuclear accident ever. A small amount of radiation was released. Without prompt action by the nuclear operators, it could have been a major disaster.**

Due to concerns about safety, Ireland is opposed to the use of nuclear energy. Several other countries–Italy, Belgium, and Germany–have stopped nuclear power development or are considering a ban on new plants. Other countries support nuclear power despite these safety issues. In November 2006, Australia decided to develop nuclear power to meet its growing demand for cleaner energy while avoiding the unsafe, polluting effects of coal. Other countries, such as Turkey and Iran, have made the decision to develop nuclear power in the near future. These countries would each like to build two or three nuclear plants in the next decade.

Three Mile Island

On March 28, 1979, Walter Cronkite, the news anchor for the CBS Evening News, began the broadcast with the following statement:

```
"It was the first step in a nuclear nightmare; as far
as we know at this hour, no worse than that. But a
government official said that a breakdown in an atomic
power plant in Pennsylvania today is probably the
worst nuclear reactor accident to date. There was no
apparent serious contamination of workers. But, a
nuclear safety group said that radiation inside the
plant is at eight times the deadly level, so strong
that after passing through a three-foot thick concrete
wall, it can be measured a mile away."
```

He was describing the core meltdown at Three Mile Island outside Harrisburg, Pennsylvania. A pump that had been sending water to help cool the nuclear fuel stopped operating. Without this cooling water, the reactor began to overheat, melting the uranium fuel and reactor equipment. Pressure built up in the reactor. To avoid an explosion, operators released radioactive gas into the atmosphere. According to most reports, no injury or illness resulted from the release of radiation at Three Mile Island. More than a dozen major health studies, including some carried out for years, showed no additional health problems for those living in the area near the power plant. The Pennsylvania Department of Health kept a database of 30,000 people who lived within five miles of the plant. After 18 years, they were unable to show any evidence of more cancer. Some reports, however, show that exposure to radioactive contamination may have caused leukemia and lung cancer deaths.

Chernobyl

Chernobyl, the worst accident in nuclear history, affected the lives of hundreds of thousands of people. They suffered forced evacuation, illness, and death. The International Atomic Energy Agency found that the design of the power plant was at fault, but human error was a major factor. The errors in the plant design were a particular problem. The plant could have a sudden increase in power when operating, making more steam and heat than it could handle. There are 12 nuclear reactors with the same design now operating in Russia and Lithuania. More than 20 other nuclear reactors with similar design problems are producing electricity in Russia, Bulgaria, Slovakia, and Armenia. Some of the equipment has been changed to improve safety, but there are serious concerns about whether these countries have the money or ability to improve

> *Chernobyl radiation is a major health threat*

Nuclear radiation from Chernobyl traveled toward Sweden, Finland, and Eastern Europe. More than 24,000 people living in the immediate area of the accident received high doses of radiation. Health researchers predict that there will be more than 17,000 future cancer cases from the radioactive contamination from Chernobyl. The area of Ukraine in the vicinity of Chernobyl is closed off, but other nearby regions are regularly examined for their radiation levels. The official check shown here took place in 2006.

safety at the remaining nuclear plants. Little is known about the condition of the nuclear reactors or safety improvements. There is also little information on new training of nuclear workers in the Chernobyl-type nuclear plants. Inadequate training led to mistakes that made the Chernobyl accident more likely. The workers had turned off an emergency cooling system that might have helped avoid the meltdown. There have been some important developments in the aftermath of the Chernobyl disaster. In 1989 private and government nuclear power plant owners established the World Association of Nuclear Operators. This organization of nuclear engineers helps share information and encourages cooperation in planning safer nuclear power. Thousands of nuclear engineers have traveled from one country to another to participate in educational meetings and training to improve nuclear safety.

Natural disasters

Safety systems are designed to shut down reactors if there is a serious emergency. An earthquake is the greatest natural threat to a nuclear power facility. The force of an earthquake may be enough to break the concrete shell of a nuclear reactor, leaking radioactivity. In July 2007, a 6.8 magnitude earthquake damaged Japan's Kashiwazaki nuclear power station, the country's largest nuclear facility. Although radiation leaks into the atmosphere and the sea were considered to be within safe limits, the power station was closed for thorough safety checks to be made. It appears that a geological fault line could extend directly underneath Kashiwazaki. This would make it make the area more likely to incur earthquake damage in the future.

Flooding and tsunamis could also damage nuclear plants. In December 2003, French nuclear safety officials declared an emergency and shut down four

> *Terrorists could target nuclear power*

A carefully planned terrorist operation may overwhelm the security guard defenses that are common at nuclear facilities, like this one. Terrorists do not need to enter the reactor core to do great damage. Attacks on transportation of fuel or nuclear waste pools could also create an environmental disaster.

nuclear plants when rain caused flooding on the Rhone River. One year later, a tsunami hit the countries of southwest Asia, killing 225,000 people. The tsunami's waves struck the atomic reactor in Kalpakkam, India, but the reactor shut down properly and withstood the waves.

Nuclear energy has the best safety record of all energy sources. National and international organizations used the accidents at Three Mile Island and Chernobyl to increase safety regulations, share information on safety issues, and prepare improved emergency plans for radiation releases. The nuclear industry is safer today, but it is not perfectly safe. An accident could occur in a nuclear reactor anywhere in the world, causing enormous damage to the surrounding population and environment. A single serious nuclear accident may produce more human, environmental, and economic costs than other energy industries may cause in decades.

The safety of certain locations may change over time. Geologists have discovered earthquake faults under nuclear power plants years after the power plants were built. Global warming may increase hurricanes and storms.

A new threat to nuclear power plants involves the risk of attack by a military force or terrorist group. As a safety measure, many of the procedures for protecting a nuclear plant are hidden deliberately from the public.

No energy source can offer all the attractive features that consumers want—low-cost, plentiful, clean, safe electricity. Clean energy sources such as renewables are more expensive and less able to meet growing electrical needs. Fossil fuels have significant risks for mine and transportation workers. They also pollute the land and air. Nuclear energy is plentiful and generally clean, but produces radioactive waste that remains poisonous for thousands of years.

 Comparison of accident statistics in primary energy production

Fuel	Fatalities	Who?	Deaths per TWy (terawatts per year) of electricity
Coal	6,400	workers	342
Hydroelectric	4,000	public	883
Natural gas	1,200	workers & public	85
Nuclear	31	workers	8

[Basis: per million MWe (megawatts electrical) operating for one year]

> *Atomic bombs have incredible explosive force*

Atomic bombs have the explosive force of millions of tons of ordinary explosives. A truck loaded with explosives has about five tons of explosive force. Even a small basic nuclear device may have 200 times that power.

What Is The Connection Between Nuclear Power And Nuclear Weapons?

At the time of explosion, an atomic bomb produces several tens of millions of degrees of heat—the temperature of the sun. Even a small explosion would kill every person within a mile of the center of the blast. In a major metropolitan area, many hundreds of thousands of people would be injured or killed within several miles of the blast. Hundreds of thousands more would be exposed to radiation that would lead to sickness and death. Debris and soil would be pulled upward into the atmosphere, returning to Earth as radioactive **fallout** and poisoning the land and water. The knowledge that is used to make nuclear electricity can also be used to produce nuclear weapons. The spread of nuclear weapons to countries is known as **proliferation**. The United States was the first country to develop an atomic bomb, with the Soviet Union close behind. France and Britain developed nuclear weapons next. China exploded its first nuclear weapon in October 1964. In the past 40 years, other countries have produced nuclear weapons, including India, Pakistan, and North Korea. The majority started their journeys with civilian nuclear energy programs.

Nuclear power as an alternative

The worldwide demand for electricity is growing. Many nations are considering alternatives to fossil fuel energy, and plans for expanding nuclear power are being studied. South Korea is building new nuclear plants. So are China, Brazil, Mexico, Argentina, and Iran. But there are serious concerns about the connection between making nuclear electrical energy and the development of nuclear weapons. To use uranium for nuclear power, it must be **enriched**. It must have at least 3-4 percent of U-235 to be used as fuel for nuclear power plants. The same technology that enriches uranium for a power plant can also be applied to enriching uranium for a weapon. To produce a bomb, uranium must be highly enriched, with 90 percent or more of U-235. In nature, uranium is primarily found as two **isotopes**, U-238 and U-235. About 99 percent of uranium is made of U-238. Most of the rest of uranium is U-235. U-235 is better for nuclear fission. Nuclear operators need to increase the percentage of U-235 in uranium to about 3-5 percent for nuclear fuel. The chemical process used to increase the percentage of U-235 in uranium is called enrichment. This is difficult and expensive. About half the cost of nuclear power is spent on uranium fuel enrichment.

In the 1960s and 1970s, countries interested in selling nuclear energy equipment and knowledge to their trading partners claimed that it was possible to expand nuclear energy while limiting the spread of nuclear weapons. That was not an accurate prediction. France, India, China, Israel, North Korea, and South Africa all developed nuclear weapons once they had civilian nuclear energy programs in place. Many of these countries started with the "Atoms for Peace" program but moved on to making atomic weapons. Of the countries that developed nuclear weapons, only one—South Africa—has eliminated its atomic weapons program.

 What do they think?

In testimony before the U.S. Senate Committee on Energy and Natural Resources in July 2006, expert Daniel B. Poneman spoke about nuclear energy:

"... The promise of nuclear power can only be fully realized if we take aggressive measures to combat the spread of nuclear weapons ... While nuclear reactors themselves are not the central problem in promoting weapons proliferation, a massive expansion of nuclear power could be accompanied by a commensurate expansion of the fuel cycle facilities capable of enriching uranium to use as nuclear power fuel and of processing out the plutonium from uranium and fission products."

> *Enriched uranium and atomic bombs*

Most of the more than 400 nuclear power plants operating in the world use enriched uranium U-235 for fuel. Highly enriched uranium is used for nuclear weapons. This photograph shows cascade tanks at a nuclear fuel enrichment plant in Kentucky.

Atoms for peace

In a 1953 speech to the United Nations, U.S. President Dwight Eisenhower tried to calm worldwide concerns about nuclear weapons by saying that nuclear energy held the key to peace. He said:

"The United States knows that if the fearful trend of atomic military buildup can be reversed, this greatest of destructive forces can be developed into a great boon, for the benefit of all mankind. The United States knows that peaceful power from atomic energy is no dream of the future. The capability already proved, is here today. Who can doubt that, if the entire body of the world's scientists and engineers had adequate amounts of fissionable material with which to test and develop their ideas, this capability would rapidly be transformed into universal, efficient and economic usage?"

In the decades after his speech, however, the development of civilian nuclear energy has been the main path that countries have used to develop nuclear weapons. Is it possible to allow nuclear power to expand without the risk of more nuclear weapons?

Nuclear Non-Proliferation Treaty

There are safeguards to limit nuclear proliferation. So far, 188 countries have agreed to follow the Nuclear Non-Proliferation Treaty, an international agreement prohibiting countries from making nuclear weapons. But countries do not always obey its rules. Some countries that have agreed to stop nuclear weapons are the same ones that sell the civilian nuclear energy equipment that has been used to make atomic bombs. The United States, Norway, the United Kingdom, Germany, France, Russia, Argentina, Australia, Niger, and Canada have sold uranium, traded nuclear equipment, and shared nuclear secrets with other countries.

Some countries, such as Israel, Pakistan, China, and India, have not signed this treaty. North Korea signed the treaty but then decided to stop cooperating with it. Under Saddam Hussein, Iraq agreed to the treaty but would not allow the United Nations to inspect its nuclear plants. Iran is currently not permitting full inspections of its nuclear facilities.

Another significant issue is that the Nuclear Non-Proliferation Treaty allows countries to develop civilian nuclear power. The treaty lets countries use the civilian technology that is the main path to weapons. Article 4 states:

1. *Nothing in this Treaty shall be interpreted as affecting the inalienable right of all Parties to the Treaty to develop research, production and use of nuclear energy for peaceful purposes without discrimination and in conformity with articles I and II of this Treaty.*

2. *All the Parties to the Treaty undertake to facilitate, and have the right to participate in, the fullest possible exchange of equipment, materials and scientific and technological information for the peaceful uses of nuclear energy. Parties to the Treaty in a position to do so shall also cooperate in contributing alone or together with other States or international organizations to the further development of the applications of nuclear energy for peaceful purposes, especially in the territories of non-nuclear-weapon States Party to the Treaty, with due consideration for the needs of the developing areas of the world.*

Although there are problems, this treaty has reduced the amount of nuclear proliferation. In the 1960s, it was presumed that 35-40 countries might have nuclear weapons by the year 2000. In 2007, there are only eight declared nuclear powers (countries that have announced and tested weapons): the United States, United Kingdom, Russia, China, France, Pakistan, India, and North Korea. Israel has not officially claimed to have nuclear weapons, but it is suspected of having as many as 200.

> *Civilian nuclear power and atomic weapons*

Many countries that have nuclear power for energy production also have nuclear weapons. With few exceptions, countries develop nuclear energy first, but the same know-how and equipment can assist countries in making nuclear weapons. This anti-nuclear protest took place in Islamabad in Pakistan.

As nuclear energy use spreads, there is worldwide concern that uranium or nuclear weapons will be more likely to get into the hands of terror groups or non-aligned and "rogue states." Rogue states have no interest in cooperating to end the spread of nuclear weapon technology. More power plants might also mean more targets for terrorists or nuclear thieves. Terrorists do not need to build a working nuclear bomb. They could also use a conventional explosion to spread radioactive material. This is known as a "dirty bomb." If this were set off in a city, it would create panic and cost millions of dollars to clean up.

Fears of nuclear proliferation and nuclear terror lead many people to prefer non-nuclear energy sources. As the supplies of oil, natural gas, and coal shrink, however, more countries will fight over the fossil fuels that remain. As water supplies in some areas become scarcer, developing hydroelectric schemes will not be possible. Can you identify places in the world where countries might fight over oil or water supplies?

> *Will Iran be the next nuclear weapon power?*
Iran expects to have two nuclear plants operating in the next few
years. These students outside a new nuclear facility in Iran are
demonstrating in support of their country's nuclear program. Europe
and the United States are concerned that Iran's civilian program will
lead to nuclear weapons, creating a political and military crisis in
the Middle East. If you were a world leader, what would you do about
Iran's nuclear energy plans?

Debating Nuclear Power

When examining the major issues, no energy source is clearly superior to another. Each one has its advantages and disadvantages. In some cases, for example, the benefits of an energy source might happen today but the problems will not be made clear for many years. Fossil fuels, for example, are available and cheap. Slowing fossil fuel development would delay getting electricity to the hundreds of millions of people who need it for health, education, agriculture, and sanitation. On the other hand, the major consequences of global warming from fossil fuels will affect Earth in ways that will not be obvious to the public for several decades, maybe longer. Global warming may seriously hurt the lives of tens of millions of people. It may lead to flooding, hunger, and the spread of disease.

How would you balance the needs and concerns of the public? The public needs electricity and would like to avoid high prices. At the same time, people want to be free from harmful air and water pollution, accidents, and hazardous wastes. They would like to avoid the dangers of nuclear terrorism and weapons. Which energy source or combination of energy sources would you select? What would you do?

Debate nuclear power!

Debate is a method of examining issues. The participants are given a topic and argue for or against it. This guide offers 3 different models for debate: two-side debating, roundtable discussion, and open forum. For a specific topic that can have a "yes" or "no" answer, it is fine to use the two-side debate model. If the topic is a more general issue, the discussion or open forum is better. Each format has rules, but participants may change them. An individual or group may judge a debate, voting on the outcome. For larger discussions, you may ask an audience which person did the best job and why.

> *Talk it out!*

Discussing the benefits and problems of nuclear power with others can help you to understand the issues better. You may find support for your opinions or learn information that persuades you to change your thinking.

Debate topics

Here are examples of specific topics. These topics focus debate on a single major point:

* Nuclear power is less expensive than coal.
* Nuclear energy will lead to harmful nuclear proliferation.
* Nuclear waste is a greater long-term threat than climate change.
* There should be one storage facility for the world's nuclear waste.

These are examples of more general topics. These topics permit a discussion on a wide range of issues:

* Nuclear energy does more good than harm.
* The International Atomic Energy Agency should be the only organization that is permitted to enrich uranium for civilian energy.
* Developing countries should use different energy sources than developed countries.
* Countries should significantly increase renewable energy.

Participants should carefully research the selected topic, making sure to form their ideas as arguments (A – R – E). They should anticipate their opponents' arguments and prepare to refute them. Depending on the rules for the event, participants may prepare notes to use during the debate. These notes should identify key points, evidence, and potential replies. Notes may include facts about the topic or arguments for debate.

 # Notes can help you win!

Factual Notes

Issue	
Problems with nuclear waste	- Poisonous for hundreds of thousands of years - No long-term safe storage - Temporary storage a target for terrorists and armed forces - New technologies that make storage safer not available for many years

[Source: Union of Concerned Scientists]

Argument Notes

My opponent says…	I say…	My opponent says…	I say…
Nuclear energy will help with global warming, reducing future pollution and protecting the population	- Waste will hurt people in the future; it is poisonous for hundreds of thousands of years - No long-term safe storage - Temporary storage a target for terrorists and armed forces	- But climate change may affect the lives of many more millions of people	- There are other technologies to help with climate change, and there are major problems storing nuclear waste

Two-side debate

One side—the *proposition* or *affirmative*—makes a case. This team must prove that the topic is more likely to be true. The *opposition* or *negative* side argues against the case. Each participant delivers a speech, with the teams taking turns. The proposition team speaks first and last. The opening proposition speaker states a case, and the first opposition speaker refutes it. Second speakers continue with their team's points and refute new points from the other side. The final speeches summarize each team's best arguments in favor of its case and against the other side. With six students, you might follow this format:

- First speaker, proposition—5 minutes
- First speaker, opposition—5 minutes
- Second speaker, proposition—5 minutes
- Second speaker, opposition—5 minutes
- Third speaker, opposition —3 minutes
- Third speaker, proposition—3 minutes

It is possible to add question and comment time by the opposing side or a class or audience during, in between, or after speeches.

Discussion

A panel discussion is designed to inform an audience. A group, or panel, of students presents and challenges ideas about an issue. Students speak for themselves and may agree or disagree with the opinions of other panel members. There is an overall time limit, perhaps 30 minutes, for the discussion. A moderator can ask questions and keep the discussion moving. Audience questions may be added afterward.

> **Let's discuss!**
>
> In a debate, the proposition side uses several major arguments to prove its case and the opposition team makes every effort to refute the case. If the proposition side convinces the audience or judging panel that its case is more likely to be true than false, it wins the debate.

Open forum

This format is effective for a class or large group. A moderator leads an open discussion on a range of topics. Audience members may present new ideas, add to what others have presented, or refute any issue. This format quickly introduces a variety of ideas.

What would you do?

From your readings and research, how would you evaluate the importance of the factors in the box below? Evaluate each factor as H – High Importance, M – Medium Importance or L – Low Importance. Some examples are completed to get you started. Which energy source or energy source mix would you prefer?

The energy decisions that are made today will affect the world for many years. No choice is ideal—each energy source has advantages and disadvantages. Nuclear power can be supported and opposed. It reduces fossil fuel pollution but produces radioactive waste; it is less expensive than renewables but may lead to nuclear weapons; it may reduce some terrorism risks but increase others. The best way to reach a conclusion about nuclear power is to examine the reasoning and evidence that support the various arguments.

Debating about nuclear power will help you understand the issues and concerns. What do you think?

Evaluating the factors

Energy Source	Access to Electricity	Cost	Pollution	Global Warming	Safety	Accidents	Hazardous Waste	Proliferation/ Military Conflict
Oil						L		
Coal								
Natural Gas		M						
Nuclear							H	
Solar			L					
Wind								
Biomass	H							
Hydro								

Find Out More

Books

- Burgan, Michael, et al. Nuclear Energy. Strongsville, Ohio: Gareth Stevens Publishing, 2002.
- Caldicott, Helen. *Nuclear Power is Not the Answer: To Global Warming or Anything Else.* New York: The New Press, 2006.
- Saunders, Nigel, and Steven Chapman. *Nuclear Energy Essentials.* Chicago: Raintree, 2005.
- Scheider, Walter. *A Serious but not Ponderous Book About Nuclear Energy.* Ann Arbor, Michigan: Cavendish Press, 2001.

Documentaries, movies, and television

- *FRONTLINE: Nuclear Reaction: Why Do Americans Fear Nuclear Power?*
  http://www.pbs.org/wgbh/pages/frontline/shows/reaction/
  Documentary film first shown on television and other online materials
- *The China Syndrome* (1979)
  American movie about reporters who film an accident at a nuclear power plant

Websites

- http://www.eere.energy.gov/consumer/information_resources/index.cfm mytopic=60001
  Hundreds of terms defined in the U.S. Department of Energy's Energy Glossary
- http://www.energyquest.ca.gov/glossary/index.html
  Hundreds of terms defined
- http://www.kathimitchell.com/elect.htm
  A teacher-created collection of more than 40 websites on electricity and science experiments about electricity for students
- http://www.ase.org/section/_audience/consumers/kids/
  Website for the Alliance to Save Energy, focused on reducing energy use throughout the world
- http://www1.eere.energy.gov/kids/
  U.S. Department of Energy—Renewable energy information

- http://www.gn.apc.org/
  GreenNet—An educational organization with information on environmental and energy issues
- http://www.teachers.ash.org.au/jmresources/energy/renewable.html
  Collection of more than 50 websites on solar, wind, hydro, biomass, geothermal, tidal, and general renewable energy
- http://www.aecl.ca/kidszone/atomicenergy
  Atomic Energy of Canada—Kids' Zone
- http://www.howstuffworks.com/nuclear-power.htm
  How nuclear power works
- http://www.iaea.org/
  International Atomic Energy Agency—United Nations organization to promote safe and secure nuclear energy
- http://www.nei.org/scienceclub/nuclearworld.html
  Nuclear Energy Institute—Information for students about nuclear energy
- http://www.nuclearfiles.org/
  The Nuclear Age Peace Foundation works to secure nuclear materials and waste and abolish nuclear weapons. The site has historical information on nuclear energy.
- http://www.ucsusa.org/clean_energy/nuclear_safety
  Union of Concerned Scientists—Information on nuclear energy and safety, renewable energy, and fossil fuels
- http://www.world-nuclear.org/
  World Nuclear Association—An organization to promote the peaceful use of nuclear energy
- http://www.prwatch.org/prwissues/2005Q1/nuke2.html
  Center for Media and Democracy—Evaluates energy information in the press
- http://www.greenpeace.org/international/
  Environmental information on a range of topics; private publications add to government and mainstream media sources

Debate resources

- Shuster, Kate, and John Meany. *Speak Out! Debate and Public Speaking in the Middle Grades.* New York: IDEA Press, 2005.
- www.middleschooldebate.com
  Comprehensive debate instruction for the classroom and competitive contests

Glossary

argument series of statements supporting one side of an issue or topic. Contains an assertion, reasoning, and evidence (A – R – E).

atom smallest piece of an element that has the chemical properties of the element

chain reaction process in nuclear fission that occurs when the splitting of one atom leads to the splitting of other atoms. The first atom releases neutrons that collide with other atoms, dividing them.

conservation saving something or using less of it. Energy conservation involves behavior changes or new technologies that reduce the use of energy.

core meltdown extreme overheating and melting that can occur in a nuclear reactor if the nuclear fuel is not cooled. It may melt through the nuclear power plant, releasing radiation to the ground and air.

element substance that cannot be made into a smaller substance by a normal chemical process

enrich to increase the percentage of an element in a mixture to create a more desirable balance for specific use, as with the percentage of U-235 in uranium

fallout when a nuclear explosion occurs and thousands of tons of soil are blown up into the atmosphere. This becomes radioactive and 'falls out' of the atmosphere back onto the ground, poisoning all living things.

fission splitting of an atom to release energy, often as heat

fossil fuel source of energy produced by the compression of earth on plant and animal matter (fossils) for millions of years. Oil, natural gas, and coal are fossil fuels.

global warming overall increase in Earth's temperature, often thought to be mainly the result of human activities, including the burning of fossil fuels that produce greenhouse gases

greenhouse gas	gas that remains in the atmosphere for a long time, creating a layer that allows heat from the Sun to pass to Earth but traps much of the heat close to the surface. This increases Earth's temperature in much the same way that the Sun's rays pass through the glass of a greenhouse and are trapped there.
hazardous waste	waste product that can burn, corrode, or poison. All energy sources produce hazardous waste.
isotope	different form of the same element. Every element has more than one isotope, but one isotope is more common than another in nature. For uranium, U-238 is much more plentiful than U-235, but does not split and produce heat as efficiently as U-235.
nonrenewable	not able to be replaced
nuclear reprocessing	after nuclear fuel has been used in nuclear reactors, the fuel can be recycled or 'reprocessed.' This procedure separates the usable parts of the fuel–uranium and plutonium. The uranium can be used for fuel but the plutonium might end up in nuclear weapons. For this reason, the UN and many governments try to reduce nuclear reprocessing.
plutonium	element produced as a result of the burning of nuclear fuel. Plutonium can be used as a fuel source for nuclear power or as the explosive core of a nuclear weapon.
proliferation	spread of something, often used to discuss the spread of nuclear weapons
radioactive	something that emits radioactivity created by changes in the nuclei of the atoms it is made from. Other things can absorb and give off this radioactivity. Radioactivity is dangerous to living things.
refutation	reply to an argument, often based on disagreement over the facts or reasoning. It can also involve the presentation of new material that disproves an opposing point.
renewable	able to be replaced. This term is used to describe energy sources that cannot be used up, such as wind and energy.
supply and demand	basic theory of economics that explains the price of a product or service based on how much is available (supply) and how much people want it (demand)
uranium	heavy metal element that is used for nuclear energy and nuclear weapons
watt	measure of electrical energy

Index